CW01082941

Original title:
The Art of Love

Author: Lan Donne
ISBN HARDBACK: 978-9916-89-148-3
ISBN PAPERBACK: 978-9916-89-149-0
ISBN EBOOK: 978-9916-89-150-6

Twilight's embrace

A hush falls soft on evening's glow,
The stars awaken, one by one,
Colors blend in a soft tableau,
As day retreats, and night begun.

Whispers dance on the cooling breeze,
Moonlit paths where shadows lie,
Rustling leaves in gentle tease,
Resources of the fading sky.

With every breath, the stillness sighs,
Night's gentle kiss on the world's face,
In twilight's arms, the spirit flies,
Finding peace in its warm embrace.

A canvas painted in dusky hues,
Dreams awaken in the fading light,
The heart, it learns, to softly choose,
To walk with grace into the night.

So linger here, where silence broods,
In twilight's grasp, let troubles cease,
For in this moment, solitude,
Brings the soul an inner peace.

Gentle Tides of Trust

On sandy shores where whispers play,
The waves caress the waiting land,
In gentle tides, the heart does sway,
With every pulse, a loving strand.

The ocean's song, a timeless tune,
It calls to all who heed its call,
Like silver beams beneath the moon,
A dance of shadows, wide and small.

With every tide, a promise flows,
Each ebb and rise, a tale retold,
In trust, the sea, its secrets shows,
Of treasures lost, and dreams of gold.

Companions shared in salty air,
The horizon stretches, bold and vast,
Together, hearts in love declare,
That moments cherished are meant to last.

As stars above begin to gleam,
The sea reflects their fragile light,
In gentle tides, we weave our dream,
Through every wave, to hold on tight.

Seasons of Sensation

Winter whispers softly, cold winds sigh,
In cozy blankets, we drift and fly.
Spring bursts forth with colors bright,
Awakening hearts, a pure delight.

Summer's laughter, warmth in the air,
Sun-kissed moments, love everywhere.
Autumn dances with a crunching sound,
Leaves beneath foot, memories abound.

Echoes of Endearment

In quiet corners, soft words bloom,
Gentle glances that chase the gloom.
Laughter lingers in shared delight,
Filling the room, igniting the night.

Promises woven in tales we tell,
In every heartbeat, we find our spell.
Each memory crafted, a treasure shared,
In the echoes of love, we are prepared.

Rhythms of Togetherness

Hand in hand, we dance through time,
With every heartbeat, our lives align.
A melody formed in joyous embrace,
In perfect harmony, we find our place.

Our laughter rings like a sweet refrain,
Through stormy weather, through joy and pain.
In every step, our shadows blend,
The rhythm of togetherness knows no end.

Unraveled Secrets

Deep in the silence, truths we find,
Whispers of life, gentle and kind.
Secrets unfold like petals of grace,
In the quiet moments, we trace our space.

Daring to share what's held inside,
With each revelation, fears subside.
In the warmth of trust, our souls ignite,
Unraveled secrets shine in the night.

Threads of Connection

In quiet whispers, hearts align,
Soft threads woven, yours and mine.
Distance may linger, but love remains,
A tapestry rich, in joys and pains.

Moments shared, like stars above,
Each memory stitched, a sign of love.
In laughter and tears, we find our way,
Threads of connection, come what may.

Strokes of Tenderness

A gentle touch, a soft embrace,
In every stroke, a sacred space.
Canvas of souls, painted bright,
With hues of kindness, pure and light.

Each word spoken, a brush of grace,
In the art of love, we find our place.
Tender moments, like petals fall,
In the garden of life, we nurture all.

A Symphony of Emotions

In the heart's chamber, melodies play,
A symphony formed in night and day.
Notes of joy, and chords of pain,
Resonating love, like gentle rain.

Every heartbeat, a rhythmic sound,
In the orchestra of life, we're all around.
Harmony forged in moments shared,
A symphony of emotions, deeply cared.

Embrace of the Infinite

In the void of night, stars ignite,
An embrace of the infinite, pure delight.
Time stands still, lost in the glow,
As the universe whispers, secrets bestow.

With every breath, we touch the divine,
In the silence, our spirits entwine.
Beyond the horizon, where dreams take flight,
We find the embrace of the infinite light.

Woven Whispers

In the quiet night so deep,
Threads of dreams begin to leap.
Whispers dance on gentle air,
Secrets tucked with tender care.

Stars align in silent grace,
Guiding hearts in their embrace.
Softly echoing the past,
Woven fabrics hold us fast.

Every stitch a tale unfolds,
Of love and hope as life molds.
In this tapestry we weave,
Bonds unbroken, we believe.

Clusters of Companionship

Beneath the shade of ancient trees,
Together we find life's sweet ease.
Clusters form, so tight and bright,
In laughter's glow, we take our flight.

Hands entwined, we share our fears,
Through stormy nights and joyful years.
A circle strong, we stand as one,
In unity, our souls are spun.

Moments cherished, never lost,
In friendship's warmth, we pay the cost.
With voices joined, we sing aloud,
A harmony that makes us proud.

Rhymes of the Heart

In the quiet, hearts will rhyme,
Echoes dance in hidden time.
Words like petals softly fall,
Secrets whispered, love's sweet call.

Every heartbeat, verse defined,
Rhythms pulse, two souls entwined.
Together crafting every line,
A sonnet made of you and mine.

Through trials faced, our stanzas grow,
In every chapter, love will show.
With ink of passion, we compose,
A tale of life that only flows.

Echoing Eternity

In the quiet of the night,
Stars above, a wondrous sight.
Echoes linger, softly call,
Reminding us we're part of all.

Time weaves in and out of grace,
Infinite dreams, we chase and trace.
Moments shared, like falling dew,
In this dance, it's me and you.

Every heartbeat sings a tune,
Underneath the silver moon.
Eternity our guiding light,
Together still, we soar in flight.

Heartbeats in Unison

In quiet spaces where whispers flow,
Two souls entwined in a soft glow.
Their heartbeats dance to a silent tune,
Under the watchful eyes of the moon.

Moments linger, sweet and rare,
Each smile shared, a gentle care.
Together they weave a fabric tight,
Embracing love's pure, radiant light.

Through storms that test, they stand their ground,
In every heartbeat, a love profound.
With trust as strong as the roots of trees,
They find their solace in the breeze.

As time flows on, their journey blends,
With every step, the world transcends.
In laughter and tears, they learn to trust,
In the beauty of love, they find they must.

Bound by a rhythm, a sacred beat,
With every pulse, their souls complete.
Together they soar, like birds in flight,
In this symphony made of pure delight.

Sinuous Paths of Romance

Winding roads through the forest deep,
Where secrets linger and shadows creep.
Love blooms in the twilight's warm hold,
A tale of passion quietly told.

Hands entwined, they share a glance,
In every moment, a fleeting chance.
With every step, they chart the course,
Driven forward by unseen force.

Stars above watch over their quest,
In the silence, their hearts find rest.
Through curves and bends, they journey far,
Guided by the soft glow of a star.

Echoes of laughter fill the air,
Creating memories beyond compare.
Where two hearts meet on a winding line,
In every heartbeat, their spirits entwine.

Lost in raptures of sweet embrace,
Time stands still in this sacred space.
With each caress, they break the night,
On sinuous paths, love takes flight.

Enchanted Interludes

In a garden where dreams softly bloom,
Every petal whispers, dispelling gloom.
Starlight dances on rippling streams,
Filling the air with magical dreams.

With every glance, the world ignites,
Colors burst in dazzling sights.
As shadows fall and fireflies rise,
They find their truth beneath the skies.

A moment captured, a stolen breath,
In the stillness, they conquer death.
Promises whispered with hearts laid bare,
In enchanted interludes, they're rare.

Time drifts like leaves in the warm breeze,
Every heartbeat a melody that frees.
Under the arch of a moonlit night,
Their souls unite, a glorious sight.

Through enchanted hours, they lose all track,
In that space, there's no turning back.
For love's sweet magic, they softly glide,
In interludes where dreams abide.

Symphony of Silences

In the night, when silence reigns,
Their love echoes, like soft refrains.
With quiet strength, they gently sway,
In a world where words can fade away.

Eyes meet in a tender gaze,
Speaking volumes in a subtle maze.
In the silence, their spirits sing,
Harmony found in everything.

A brush of hands, electric spark,
Illuminating the softening dark.
In stillness, they hear the soul's call,
In symphony, they rise, they fall.

Through whispered breaths, they share their fears,
In the absence of sound, they find the years.
Every heartbeat, a note in the night,
A symphony born from love's pure light.

When all is quiet, and moments freeze,
In the calm, they find their ease.
Together they dance, hearts entwined,
In a silent rhythm, beautifully aligned.

Waves of Desire

Waves crash against the shore,
Whispers of longing at the core.
Each tide pulls at my soul,
Drawing me closer, making me whole.

The sun dips low and glows,
A fiery kiss where passion flows.
Salt in the air, a spark so bright,
Guiding our hearts into the night.

Soft sand beneath our feet,
Time stands still, so bittersweet.
Every wave carries our dreams,
Together we flow, in silken seams.

Moonlight bathes the ocean wide,
In this moment, there's no need to hide.
Waves of desire, endless and free,
Forever entwined, just you and me.

As the stars begin to blink,
We sway gently, lose ourselves in the ink.
A canvas painted with love's embrace,
Waves of desire, our sacred space.

Radiance of Togetherness

In the morning glow, we rise,
With the sun painting the skies.
Together we walk hand in hand,
A bond unbroken, beautifully planned.

Laughter dances on cool breezes,
In every shared smile, the heart eases.
Moments cherished, both big and small,
In the radiance of love, we have it all.

Side by side, through thick and thin,
Strength in unity, together we win.
Every heartbeat sings a song,
In this togetherness, we belong.

Underneath the starry dome,
With you, my heart has found its home.
Together we shine, our spirits bright,
In the radiance of love, we're alight.

As the day turns into night,
With each embrace, everything feels right.
Hand in hand, we'll face each test,
In the radiance of togetherness, we are blessed.

Shadows of Sweetness

In twilight's hush, secrets unfold,
Shadows dance, stories untold.
Wrapped in warmth, beneath the trees,
A symphony whispered in every breeze.

With you, the world fades away,
In tender moments, we gently sway.
Sweetness lingers in every glance,
In the shadows, we find our chance.

Fingers intertwine like vines,
In this embrace, everything aligns.
Echoes of laughter fill the air,
In shadows of sweetness, joy we share.

The night wraps us in its veil,
With every heartbeat, love won't fail.
In quiet corners where dreams collide,
In shadows of sweetness, we abide.

As the stars light up the sky,
Together we'll soar, together we'll fly.
In whispered promises, hearts find rest,
In shadows of sweetness, we've been blessed.

Dreamscape of Us

In the realm where dreams take flight,
A canvas woven with pure delight.
Every heartbeat echoes our song,
In this dreamscape, we both belong.

Glistening stars weave through the night,
Guiding us gently, a cherished sight.
With every wish, we reach for more,
In this land of us, there's always more.

The horizon blurs, time stands still,
An endless wonder, a gentle thrill.
Together we chase the starlit streams,
In the dreamscape of us, we're alive in dreams.

As the moonlight cradles our dreams,
Each moment, a spark, or so it seems.
With open hearts, we dance and sway,
In this dreamscape, forever we'll play.

Awakening softly, we hold what's true,
In the magic of dreams, it's me and you.
Forever entwined, in every breath,
In the dreamscape of us, love knows no death.

Tapestry of Togetherness

In threads of gold and silver spun,
We weave our dreams, two souls as one.
Each stitch a story, bright and new,
In this embrace, I find the true.

With laughter's echo, joy we share,
In every moment, love laid bare.
Through storms and sunshine, hand in hand,
Together we rise, together we stand.

The colors blend, a vibrant hue,
In this tapestry, I find you.
Through every trial, we will grow,
In the warmth of love, our spirits glow.

A silent promise, soft yet clear,
In every heartbeat, you are near.
With every thread that intertwines,
The fabric of love, perfectly aligns.

In the twilight's glow, we'll reflect,
On all the moments we collect.
For in our hearts, forever stays,
The tapestry of love always displays.

Harmonies of the Heart

In whispers soft, the melodies play,
Notes of affection, guiding our way.
With every heartbeat, a rhythm grows,
In the dance of life, love freely flows.

We sing the songs our spirits know,
In harmony, through highs and low.
A gentle cadence beneath the stars,
Our hearts in sync, no distance far.

Through laughter's chorus, pain's refrain,
We find the strength to break the chains.
In every silence, a song remains,
Echoing love through joys and pains.

The music swells, a sweet embrace,
In every note, I see your face.
Together, harmonies we compose,
A symphony that gently grows.

As twilight lingers, let us sway,
In this love song, forever stay.
For in our souls, the music's part,
Together we sing, harmonies of the heart.

Paintbrush of Passion

With colors bright, I stroke the line,
Each hue a memory, yours and mine.
In swirls and splashes, love's spirit gleams,
On canvas wide, we chase our dreams.

With every stroke, a story told,
In shades of red, in strokes of gold.
The paintbrush dances, hand in hand,
Creating worlds where hearts expand.

Brush of desire, soft and bold,
In every hue, our love unfolds.
Though shadows may fall and colors fade,
In this masterpiece, memories laid.

As twilight falls, the canvas glows,
In every corner, my passion shows.
Together, we paint, our spirits free,
A vibrant work of you and me.

In the gallery of our design,
With every stroke, our souls entwine.
Forever captured, this love's art,
A paintbrush of passion, igniting the heart.

Reflections in a Shared Gaze

In your eyes, I see my soul,
A world of wonder, making me whole.
With each glance, stories unfold,
Reflections deep, more precious than gold.

The silence speaks in whispers sweet,
In every moment, our hearts meet.
A shared gaze that knows no bounds,
In this connection, love resounds.

Through layers of dreams and hopes combined,
In your gaze, my heart's defined.
With every look, the truth we find,
A mirror that leaves no soul behind.

In twilight's peace, we linger long,
In the shared gaze, we both belong.
With every beat, our spirits rise,
Reflections glowing in the skies.

So let us stay in this embrace,
Where love and time both find their place.
In the depths of your eyes, I see,
Reflections of love, pure and free.

Starlit Conversations

Under the moonlit sky, we share dreams,
Whispers of hopes float on gentle beams.
Stars twinkle above, like secrets in air,
In this quiet moment, we lay our hearts bare.

Laughter dances softly, brushing the night,
Every word spoken feels perfectly right.
Time stands still as our souls intertwine,
In the symphony of silence, your hand in mine.

The universe listens to our soft confide,
In the vastness of space, there's nowhere to hide.
We share tales of wonder, of losses, of gains,
Each note of our laughter, a magical chain.

Gazing at galaxies, lost in their glow,
Each twinkling star holds the stories we sow.
In this starlit haven, where love lights the way,
We find in each other what words cannot say.

So let us forever hold on to this night,
In the tapestry woven, stitched tight by twilight.
For in starlit conversations, our spirits will soar,
Magic unspoken, forever in store.

Journey of Two

Hand in hand, we embark on this quest,
Through valleys and peaks, we find our rest.
With every step, new wonders unfurl,
In this journey of two, we explore the world.

Paths may diverge, but hearts stay aligned,
In the dance of the day, our souls are entwined.
With laughter as our compass, love as our guide,
Across rivers and deserts, we take life in stride.

The sun paints the sky in hues of our dreams,
As we gather the moments, like shimmering beams.
Every road we travel is rich with delight,
In the warmth of your gaze, the darkness takes flight.

We gather the memories like treasures in time,
Singing the verses of our shared rhyme.
No distance can sever the bond that we hold,
In the journey of two, our story unfolds.

With stars overhead and the moon as our fan,
Together we wander, hand in hand we span.
For life's not a race but a beautiful flow,
In this journey of two, together we grow.

Timeless Whispers

In the hush of the night, secrets are shared,
Timeless whispers echo, showing we cared.
With each soft murmur, a story untold,
Our hearts beat in rhythm, a bond to behold.

Memories linger like shadows of light,
Every promise we made feels so infinite.
In the depths of our silence, we find our way,
Through echoes of yesterday, forever we'll stay.

The clock ticks but quietly, time bows its head,
In the warmth of your gaze, all fears are shed.
A tapestry woven from laughter and sighs,
In this sanctuary, our affection will rise.

With hands gently clasped, we cherish the now,
In whispers that linger, we make our vow.
For time is an ocean, vast and profound,
In the ebb and the flow, our love will be found.

So let us remain in this tender embrace,
Where timeless whispers fill each empty space.
For within every heartbeat, each moment we share,
Lies the language of love, as silent as air.

Seasons of Affection

In spring's gentle blush, our love bloomed anew,
Petals of laughter danced in skies so blue.
With every soft breeze, sweet moments arise,
In the season of warmth, our spirits did fly.

Summer's embrace wraps us, golden and bright,
Longer days filled with joy, hearts taking flight.
We explore sun-kissed paths, hand in hand we roam,
Every sunset whispers, together we're home.

As autumn leaves fall, we gather the gold,
Seasons of affection, warm stories unfold.
Crimson hues blanket the earth in a quilt,
In this cozy embrace, our hearts will not wilt.

Winter arrives with its soft, gentle hug,
A quiet reflection, love's warmest rug.
Through frost-kissed windows, we share fireside dreams,
In the season of quiet, our love gently gleams.

Each season a chapter, a story to tell,
In the book of our lives, we flourish and swell.
Through the cycles of time, come sunshine or rain,
In these seasons of affection, our love will remain.

Verses of Vulnerability

In shadows where fears often dwell,
Whispers of doubt begin to swell.
Hearts adorned with scars and grace,
Yearning for love's warm embrace.

Beneath the armor, we hide so deep,
Dreams fractured, but still we keep.
Breaking our paths to heal the soul,
Finding strength to feel whole.

Letting go of pretenses bright,
Hoping for dawn after the night.
With every tear, we carve a way,
Towards brighter, braver days.

Trust is a fragile, shimmering thread,
Binding the hearts where worries bled.
In silence, we share unspoken fears,
Building bridges across the years.

In the echo of our silent cries,
An orchestra of truths underlies.
Embracing the flaws, the rawness shown,
In vulnerability, we are never alone.

Symphony of Hearts

In every beat, a story unfolds,
Melodies of dreams, both shy and bold.
Each pulse a rhythm, pure and sweet,
Dancing together, two souls meet.

Harmonies blend in electric light,
Guiding us softly through the night.
With every glance, a silent song,
In this union, where we belong.

The crescendo rises with whispered prayers,
Cacophony fades as love declares.
Notes intertwined, our journey starts,
Creating a symphony of hearts.

In quiet moments, the music swells,
Echoing secrets that time compels.
Together we rise, together we fall,
In this symphony, we embrace it all.

As the finale draws gentle and near,
Each note engraved, forever clear.
In the silence, where dreams impart,
Rests the melody of every heart.

The Language of Touch

Fingers brush like soft-spun dreams,
Creating warmth in gentle seams.
A language written without a word,
In subtle glances, love is stirred.

With every caress, stories ignite,
Unraveling mysteries, day turns night.
The pulse of connection, tender and true,
In the silence, just me and you.

Soft as petals, fierce as fire,
Touch awakens hidden desire.
In the curve of a hand, the arch of a back,
Every gesture, a love-filled act.

Wrapped in presence, we lose our fears,
Sinking into rhythms, through the years.
In embrace where silence speaks loud,
We find solace, solace unbowed.

With each heartbeat, an echo we feel,
The language of touch becomes our seal.
Two bodies, one story, forever we'll weave,
In whispers of skin, love will believe.

Sculpted Promises

In carved wood and marbled stone,
Promises whispered, never alone.
Sculpted dreams in every line,
A masterpiece, yours and mine.

Chiseling doubts with hearts of trust,
Molding hopes from passionate lust.
In every curve, a tale resides,
Of union forged where love abides.

Through storms that threaten to take their toll,
We etch our vows into the soul.
A sculpture stands against the tide,
In crafted strength, we confide.

Time may weather, and shadows grow,
Yet in these figures, our love will flow.
Each crack and crevice tells our worth,
In sculpted promises, joy gives birth.

So let us carve with hands and heart,
Together forever, we shall not part.
In the gallery of life, our love on display,
Sculpted promises, come what may.

Canvas of Affection

On a canvas bright and wide,
Love's colors blend and glide.
Gentle strokes of light and shade,
In this art, our hearts conveyed.

Every hue tells a tale,
Of laughter, joy, and shared travail.
Brush in hand, we paint our dreams,
In this vibrant world, love beams.

Together, we create the scene,
Where passion flows, and hearts convene.
Each moment framed, a timeless piece,
In this gallery, our hearts find peace.

With every touch, we grow, we learn,
In the warmth of love, we brightly burn.
A masterpiece of hope and grace,
In each other's arms, we find our place.

As the colors dance and sway,
Forever in this art we stay.
Canvas of affection, bold and true,
A story painted just for me and you.

Whispers in the Heart

In the silence, soft and clear,
Whispers of love, I long to hear.
A gentle breeze that calls your name,
Filling my soul with a warm flame.

Through the night, secrets we share,
Dreams unfolding, a tender care.
With every sigh, our hearts align,
In this dance, your heart is mine.

Moments linger like a sigh,
In your gaze, I find the sky.
Whispers float on moonlit beams,
Carving out our sweetest dreams.

Held in time, a fleeting glance,
In this rhythm, we take a chance.
Soft and sweet, our hearts unfold,
Whispers in the dark, love untold.

Each heartbeat, a love song played,
In your arms, my fears allayed.
With every whisper, love portrayed,
In this quiet, our romance laid.

Chasing the Sunset Together

Hand in hand, we roam the shore,
Chasing sunsets, wanting more.
Golden hues paint the sky,
In this moment, we learn to fly.

As the sun dips low and wide,
We leave our worries far behind.
With every wave, a memory made,
In this twilight, our hearts are swayed.

The horizon whispers sweet and low,
Guiding us where love can grow.
Each step taken, side by side,
In this journey, our hearts confide.

Colors merge in a soft embrace,
The sunset's kiss, a perfect grace.
Together, we watch the day depart,
Chasing the sunset, heart to heart.

In the glow of the dying light,
We find our way, our paths unite.
Chasing dreams as the night draws near,
In every sunset, I hold you dear.

Brushstrokes of Devotion

With each stroke, a tale unfolds,
In vibrant colors, love beholds.
Brushes dance like hearts in tune,
Painting our love beneath the moon.

In every hue, a promise lies,
A canvas bright, where passion flies.
From deep cerulean to bright gold,
Our story's painted, bold and bold.

Every blend, a soft embrace,
In this artwork, we find our place.
With fervent strokes and patient hands,
Devotion flows, like silent sands.

Together, we create, we dream,
In every line, a lover's theme.
Through thick and thin, this bond we share,
In brushstrokes of devotion, love laid bare.

With every piece, our hearts reflect,
A masterpiece, love's true architect.
In this gallery, forever we'll dwell,
In brushstrokes bright, our hearts compel.

Radiance of Resonance

In the dawn's gentle light,
Voices mingle, take flight.
Melodies weave in the air,
Notes of truth, soft and fair.

A chorus of hearts aligned,
Whispers of dreams intertwined.
Each sound a spark, a flare,
Together, we rise and dare.

Echoes dance through the trees,
A symphony carried by breeze.
In the silence, we find grace,
A radiant, warm embrace.

From shadows we draw near,
Unveiling what we hold dear.
As laughter fills the space,
Harmony finds its place.

Bright reflections we share,
Moments cherished, beyond compare.
In the twilight's glowing glaze,
We celebrate with our gaze.

Soft Echoes of Affinity

In whispered winds, we find,
Echoes of the heart, unlined.
Gentle touches, soft and true,
A language shared by me and you.

Through quiet paths we roam,
Familiarity feels like home.
In every glance, a story hums,
A truth that softly becomes.

Hearts beat in tender sync,
Boundless thoughts, no need to think.
Within the stillness, bonds ignite,
Illuminating the night.

With every laugh, a wall breaks,
A tapestry woven from heartaches.
In shared smiles, we uncover,
The sacred ties of sister, brother.

So let the soft echoes play,
Guiding us through night and day.
In harmony, our spirits rise,
Affinity beneath endless skies.

Journeys in Sync

Beneath the stars we gather close,
Paths entwined, we feel engrossed.
With each step, a rhythm flows,
In this dance, our spirit glows.

Each mile traveled, a bond formed,
Through the storms, we've all warmed.
With laughter shared and tears cried,
In every journey, side by side.

The compass points to dreams anew,
With courage found in me and you.
Exploring realms both near and far,
Guided always by our star.

In moments paused, we reflect,
On the love that we select.
Each memory, a thread so fine,
Woven through the hands of time.

As we walk this endless road,
Crafting stories, shedding load.
Together in the vast expanse,
Life unfolds in a tender dance.

The Pulse of Passion

In the heart's resounding beat,
Lies a fire, pure and sweet.
Embers kindle, hearts align,
In every look, a sign divine.

With fervor bright, we create,
A tapestry we celebrate.
Each moment sparks the flame,
In this wild and wondrous game.

Love ignites the darkest night,
Guiding us toward the light.
In the chase of every dream,
Together, we build and beam.

Through struggles, we hold tight,
Reflections shared in the twilight.
With every breath, we affirm,
A passion that will always burn.

As dawn breaks, we arise,
With courage etched in our eyes.
In the pulse of life, we live,
For in love's sway, we truly give.

Embracing the Unknown

In shadows deep, we tread anew,
Set sail on seas without a clue.
With every step, we stretch our wings,
To find the joy that adventure brings.

A whisper of hope in the hidden night,
Guides us onward, beyond our sight.
We'll face the storms and dance in the rain,
Together we'll thrive, through loss and gain.

With hearts entwined, we dare to explore,
The wonders that lie behind each door.
For in the unknown, our spirits ignite,
And darkness transforms into brilliant light.

As paths diverge, we hold on tight,
With courage fueling our shared flight.
In the midst of fear, we choose to stand,
Together forever, hand in hand.

So let us embrace what we cannot see,
In the dance of life, you and me.
With dreams alight and voices strong,
We'll weave our tale, where we belong.

Wings of Wild Affection

In evening glow, our laughter soars,
On wind-swept hills, love gently pours.
With every glance, our spirits align,
In this dance of hearts, your soul is mine.

We leap like birds, unbound and free,
Chasing the sun through the ancient trees.
With whispers sweet, we touch the sky,
Wings of wild affection, you and I.

The stars bear witness to our delight,
As day surrenders to the velvet night.
In this embrace, we lose all fear,
For love's true magic is always near.

We'll weather storms, with laughter and grace,
Together we'll find our sacred space.
With every heartbeat, our love takes flight,
A journey painted in colors so bright.

So let us dance in this wild embrace,
In every corner of this sacred space.
With wings spread wide and spirits high,
Forever together, you and I.

Whirls of Whimsy

In fanciful spins, where dreams take flight,
We dance with shadows, twirl with light.
A sprinkle of laughter, a dash of cheer,
In whirls of whimsy, we disappear.

Through fields of daisies, we chase the breeze,
With giggles and grins, our worries freeze.
Each moment a treasure, a playful sign,
In this world of magic, your hand in mine.

With colors blooming in riotous hue,
We skip through the meadows, just me and you.
Every glance a promise, every step a song,
In the whirl of joy, we truly belong.

Beneath the stars, we twinkle and glow,
With secrets whispered and hearts all aglow.
In the realm of dreams where wonders unfurl,
We dance through the night, two souls in a whirl.

And when the morning brings light anew,
We'll chase the sun with hearts so true.
For in this life, every twist and turn,
Holds magic and whimsy for hearts that yearn.

Books Unread Together

In dusty corners, stories lie,
Pages untouched, waiting to fly.
With fingers tracing the worn-out spine,
We dream of worlds where hearts entwine.

Each unread tale a whispered sigh,
Ink yet to dance, under starlit sky.
In quiet moments, we share the thrill,
Of adventures waiting, hearts to fill.

With every chapter, new paths we'll take,
Together we'll journey, for memory's sake.
In the margins, we'll write our own,
Creating a world that's ours alone.

So let us gather these tales of old,
As mysteries unfold and visions bold.
In stories shared, we find our grace,
In pages unwritten, we'll find our place.

With every book, a bond we weave,
In words unspoken, we truly believe.
For in those tomes, with you beside,
We write our future, a wondrous ride.

Timeless Touches

In whispers soft, the breezes play,
Carrying scents of yesterday.
Each moment held, a breath held tight,
A dance of shadows, day and night.

Hand in hand, we roam the past,
Left footprints in the sand so fast.
With every glance, a spark ignites,
Eternal echoes of our nights.

Between the pages, time will fold,
Stories shared, in heartbeats bold.
Each touch a language, pure and true,
A timeless bond, just me and you.

The sun descends, the stars arise,
Guiding dreams beneath vast skies.
Moments linger, whispers sweet,
In every heartbeat, love's retreat.

Through all the changes, seasons pass,
Our laughter glows like polished glass.
With timeless touches, we ignite,
A tapestry of love, pure light.

Shadows of Devotion

In quiet corners, shadows creep,
A loyal vow, a love so deep.
With every sigh, a promise made,
In whispered halls, our hearts conveyed.

Through storms that swirl and skies of gray,
Your light will guide, come what may.
In gentle moments, fears dissolve,
Shadows dance, as we evolve.

Our hands entwined, we face the night,
In darkest hours, find our light.
Each heartbeat echoes, strong and clear,
Shadows of love, always near.

With every test, our bond won't break,
In silence shared, our souls awake.
Through life's pathways, slow and fast,
We build a future, hold the past.

In shadows deep, our dreams take flight,
With whispered love, we chase the night.
Forever bound, in heart's devotion,
Two souls as one, an endless ocean.

The Warmth Between Us

In morning light, our laughter glows,
A gentle warmth that ever flows.
Wrapped in comfort, hand in hand,
Together here, we bravely stand.

The world outside may race and spin,
But in this space, our dreams begin.
With every glance, love's ember heats,
In quiet moments, our heartbeats.

Through stormy skies and sunny days,
In woven threads of soft sunrays.
We'll face the winds, whatever calls,
With warmth between us, love enthralls.

In stolen glances, time stands still,
A sacred trust, a steadfast will.
We'll chase the stars, with hearts on fire,
In every breath, a shared desire.

No distance vast can dim this light,
For in your eyes, the world feels right.
Through every trial, safe and sound,
The warmth between us, forever found.

Crafting Moments

With open hearts, we share our days,
In simple joys, love's gentle ways.
Crafting moments, strong and bright,
In every laugh, we find our light.

Painting sunsets, hand in hand,
A masterpiece that life has planned.
Through every brushstroke, colors blend,
Creating memories, love transcends.

In the quiet, magic brews,
With whispered words, a friendship true.
Each passing hour, a gift bestowed,
Crafting moments, our love, the road.

Through laughter shared and tears we shed,
In each embrace, our fears are fed.
We weave the night, we spin the day,
In crafting moments, come what may.

Each heartbeat sings an untold tale,
As we set forth, we will not fail.
In life's design, our story flows,
Crafting moments, as our love grows.

Fragments of Forever

In whispers lost, the shadows dance,
Memories linger, a fleeting glance.
Echoes of laughter, soft and bright,
Fragments of dreams in the still of night.

Time drips slowly, like melting gold,
Stories untold in the hearts we hold.
Each moment a shard of radiant light,
Fading yet vivid, a bittersweet sight.

A tapestry woven with threads so fine,
Moments entwined in a sacred line.
The warmth of love that time can't sever,
Holding on tight to fragments of forever.

Each heartbeat, a note in a timeless song,
In the quiet spaces where we belong.
Through the seasons, we quietly roam,
Chasing reflections that lead us home.

In twilight's embrace, where silence reigns,
We gather the pieces, despite the pains.
Each fragment a treasure, a glimmer they bring,
In the vastness of time, our spirits take wing.

Tapestry of Togetherness

Strands of laughter, colors blend,
Weaving stories, hand in hand.
In every moment, a thread we weave,
Tapestry rich in what we believe.

Through trials faced, and joys we share,
United in love, a bond so rare.
Each stitch a promise, each knot a vow,
Together we flourish, here and now.

In evening's glow, we find our place,
With every smile, a warm embrace.
Across the canvas, life's motifs shine,
Transforming shadows into design.

With every heartbeat, our world expands,
From distant shores to familiar lands.
In the gentle silence, connection grows,
A fabric of hearts that forever flows.

In the dance of time, we twirl and sway,
Crafting our story, come what may.
In this tapestry bright, we ever stand,
Woven in love, a united strand.

Hues of Harmony

In the morning light, colors arise,
Painting the skies, where freedom lies.
Brushstrokes of kindness, splashes of grace,
Hues of harmony fill every space.

Through gentle whispers and soft caress,
Nature sings tunes of pure happiness.
The blues of the ocean, the greens of the trees,
A symphony crafted by the tender breeze.

Upon the canvas of a fleeting day,
Moments glimmer, in shades of play.
Each color a heartbeat, a voice unheard,
In the language of beauty, we find the word.

With every sunset, a palette glows,
The warmth of the red, where compassion flows.
In twilight's embrace, peace settles near,
Hues of harmony cradle each tear.

Together we paint, with colors so bold,
A masterpiece written in stories untold.
United in spirit, we'll find a way,
To blend our hues until the break of day.

Chords of Connection

In the quiet night, a melody hums,
Strumming the heart, where the magic comes.
Chords of connection, a rhythm so pure,
Binding our souls, love's sweetest cure.

Every note a whisper, every beat a sigh,
In the world's embrace, we reach for the sky.
With laughter as harmony, tears as the bass,
We dance through life, in this sacred space.

From distant echoes to close-knit ties,
The sound of our journey softly flies.
In every heartbeat, we share the song,
A chorus of life, where we all belong.

Through valleys low and mountains high,
We'll strum the strings as the moments fly.
In each frame of time, a refrain we find,
Chords of connection, forever entwined.

As dawn breaks anew, let our music soar,
In each other's arms, we are never poor.
For in this duet, we rise and shine,
Chords of connection, yours and mine.

Sculpting Dreams Together

In the quiet of the night, we start,
Molding visions from the heart.
With every touch, we shape our fate,
Creating worlds, it's never too late.

Laughter weaves in every design,
A tapestry of dreams entwined.
With hands united, we carve each plan,
Building beauty, as only we can.

Every whispered wish takes flight,
Guiding our souls into the light.
Together we rise, with hopes that gleam,
Sculpting our future, living the dream.

Through trials, we find a way,
Chasing shadows into the day.
In every challenge, side by side,
Sculpting dreams, our hearts open wide.

As the stars above us gleam,
We continue to chase our dream.
In this dance, forever we stand,
Sculpting dreams, hand in hand.

Sunsets and Sweet Nothings

As the sun dips low in the sky,
Soft whispers float, as the day says goodbye.
Golden hues paint the evening light,
In each other's arms, everything feels right.

Moments shared, like petals fall,
We speak sweet nothings, enveloped in thrall.
Time slows down, as colors bend,
In sunsets, our hearts begin to mend.

With every laugh, shadows fade,
In this twilight, memories are made.
Together, we dream of distant shores,
In the warmth of dusk, love forever soars.

Hand in hand, we walk the strand,
Feeling the grains of the soft, warm sand.
Each heartbeat echoes in the air,
Sunsets and sweet nothings, a love so rare.

As stars awaken to light the night,
We find solace in each other's sight.
With tender glances, our souls ignite,
In the embrace of love, everything feels right.

Tides of Togetherness

Waves whisper secrets to the shore,
A rhythm of love we can't ignore.
In the ebb and flow, we find our place,
Tides of togetherness, a warm embrace.

Each moment shared, a treasure we keep,
In the depths of our hearts, love runs deep.
Like the ocean, vast and wide,
In the journey of life, we'll always ride.

With each rise and fall, we grow,
Through storms and calms, our bond will glow.
Together we weather the ever-changing sea,
Tides of togetherness, just you and me.

Hand in hand, we face each wave,
Finding strength in the love we crave.
In the currents of life, we shall thrive,
Together, forever, we are alive.

As the sun sets over the ocean's crest,
In this adventure, we are truly blessed.
With each tide that rolls across this land,
Together we stand, and hand in hand.

Letters Beneath the Stars

Under the canopy of the night,
Whispers echo, a soft delight.
With each letter, our hearts entwine,
Beneath the stars, your hand in mine.

Ink on paper, a dance of words,
Like magic spell, our love is stirred.
In the silence, secrets unfold,
Each letter penned, a story told.

As constellations twinkle bright,
Our dreams take flight, like birds in flight.
In this moment, time stands still,
With each promise, our hearts fulfill.

Underneath the heavens so wide,
In every word, there's love and pride.
Together we'll write our endless tale,
Letters beneath the stars, we'll prevail.

As the night fades to dawn's embrace,
With letters sweet, our love we'll trace.
In the light of day, may it always last,
Letters beneath the stars, our love steadfast.

Colors of Connection

In shades of laughter, we intertwine,
Threads of joy, both yours and mine.
A canvas painted with vibrant hues,
Each stroke a story, each moment, a muse.

Through whispered secrets beneath the stars,
We trace our dreams, erasing the scars.
The palette of friendship, forever it glows,
In every heartbeat, our bond truly flows.

With every sunset, our colors blend,
A masterpiece crafted, where hearts don't end.
Every shade speaks of love and grace,
In this tapestry woven, we find our place.

Amidst life's chaos, we boldly stand,
United in spirit, hand in hand.
The colors of connection, pure and bright,
Illuminate the path, guiding our flight.

In each moment shared, a rainbow ignites,
The beauty of souls, in dazzling lights.
Together we flourish, together we sing,
In this world of colors, our spirits take wing.

Dance of Longing

Under the pale moon, shadows sway,
Whispers of dreams inviting the fray.
A melody lingers, soft and sweet,
As hearts beat softly to an unseen beat.

From afar I watch, your grace unfold,
Each twirl a story, each move so bold.
In the silence, longing takes its place,
A tender ache, a soft embrace.

With every glance, my spirit yearns,
In the dance of longing, passion burns.
A waltz of wishes beneath the stars,
Drawing us closer, no matter how far.

Every moment shared in the twilight's glow,
Inviting the stars to witness our flow.
In this rapture, time drifts away,
As we spin together, come what may.

In this dance of secrets, souls entwine,
To the rhythm of hearts, divine design.
With each step, we find our way,
In the dance of longing, forever we'll stay.

Sculpting Memories

With gentle hands, I mold the clay,
Each touch a heartbeat, in the fray.
Carving moments, both big and small,
In the art of history, we rise and fall.

Beneath the surface, stories hide,
In the vessel of time, they confide.
A whisper of laughter, a tear we shed,
In this sculpture of life, our truths are bred.

From whispers of youth to the wisdom of age,
We shape our legacy, page by page.
Every crack and line, a chapter told,
In the kiln of dreams, our spirits unfold.

The beauty of memories, both fragile and bold,
Each piece a treasure, more precious than gold.
Mosaics of laughter, fragments of pain,
Sculpting our essence, time's gentle gain.

As the years flow by, the form may change,
Yet the heart of this art will never estrange.
In the gallery of moments, we forever roam,
Sculpting memories, we find our home.

Petals on the Wind

Softly they flutter, like whispers of spring,
Petals on the wind, a delicate fling.
Carried by breezes, they dance through the air,
A journey of beauty, beyond compare.

Each color a story, a wish set free,
In the garden of dreams, where blossoms decree.
A tapestry woven with love and delight,
Petals on the wind, a wondrous sight.

When the sun smiles down, they twirl and soar,
Painting the sky, a canvas to explore.
With the heart as their guide, they drift away,
In the arms of the wind, they find their play.

Through valleys and mountains, they wander and roam,
Each petal a traveler, finding a home.
In the symphony of nature, their voices rise,
Petals on the wind, beneath endless skies.

As seasons shift, their journey won't cease,
Carried by stories, they whisper of peace.
In every flutter, a moment to mend,
Petals on the wind, our souls they transcend.

Chasing Echoes

Through silent woods, whispers play,
Shadows linger, fading away.
Footsteps soft on ancient ground,
Chasing echoes yet unheard sounds.

Moonlight dances, flickers bright,
Guiding dreams into the night.
In every rustle, secrets hide,
Lost in the maze, time's gentle tide.

Voices murmur, calling near,
Fragments of hope, tinged with fear.
With every breath, the past entwines,
In the heart's chamber, memory shines.

Fleeting moments, lost in flight,
Chasing echoes, seeking light.
Through the darkness, we pursue,
The whispers that once felt so true.

In twilight's arms, we'll find our way,
Chasing echoes till break of day.
With every beat, the chase renewed,
In the silence, our dreams are brewed.

Serenade of Souls

In twilight's glow, two hearts collide,
A serenade where secrets hide.
Whispered promises softly spoken,
In the silence, bonds unbroken.

Stars above twinkle like dreams,
Illuminating tender seams.
Each note played in harmony,
Binding souls, a symphony.

Gentle breezes carry our tune,
Dancing lightly beneath the moon.
In every glance, a story holds,
Love's enchantment, timeless golds.

As shadows blend in sweet embrace,
We find our rhythm, our own space.
With every heartbeat, the music swells,
In the serenade, our longing dwells.

Together we weave a tapestry,
A serenade of you and me.
In each moment, our spirits soar,
In love's symphony, forevermore.

Palette of Passion

Brush strokes vibrant, colors bright,
On canvas dreams ignite the night.
With every hue, emotions flow,
A palette of passion, love's warm glow.

Sparks of red, desire's flame,
Whispered secrets, never the same.
Soft blues serenade the heart,
In every shade, a work of art.

Golden yellows, laughter gleams,
Filling the air with vibrant dreams.
Greens of harmony, deep and true,
Life's tangled threads, me and you.

In every brush stroke, stories unfold,
A dance of feelings, brave and bold.
From light to shadows, we find our way,
In the palette of passion, forever stay.

Underneath skies painted gray,
We'll find our colors come what may.
As long as the heart knows how to feel,
In the palette of passion, love is real.

Dance of Desire

In the midnight glow, bodies sway,
A dance of desire, come what may.
With every step, the world will fade,
In this moment, our fears laid.

Eyes entwined in a fiery gaze,
Lost in the rhythm, a passionate craze.
Fingers trace paths along the skin,
In the silence, where love begins.

Heartbeats echo, a pulse so strong,
In this dance, we both belong.
The music whispers secrets sweet,
In each embrace, our souls complete.

Twisting, turning, we find our place,
In the dance of desire, time we chase.
With every twirl, the longing grows,
In this ballet, only passion knows.

Until the dawn breaks, we'll fly high,
In the dance of desire, you and I.
As shadows stretch and sunlight warms,
We'll keep dancing through life's storms.

Glimmers of Eternity

In twilight's hush, the stars ignite,
Whispers of dreams take fragile flight.
The moon ascends, a silent guide,
Casting shadows where hopes abide.

Moments bloom like flowers rare,
Time stands still in the evening air.
Fleeting glances, hearts entwined,
Echoes linger, softly defined.

Infinite skies in shades of blue,
Every wish a promise true.
In the dusk, we find our way,
Through the night, we yearn and sway.

With every breath, a tale unfolds,
Secrets shared, yet still untold.
The dance of time, both fast and slow,
In the stillness, love can grow.

A flicker in the endless dark,
Where paths converge, igniting spark.
In the glow, we dare to dream,
Finding solace in moonbeam gleam.

Fables of Longing

In a world of tales, I seek the truth,
Woven whispers of my youth.
Every story echoes clear,
Craving dreams that draw us near.

Time flows gently like a stream,
Each heartbeat a lingering dream.
Fables told through ancient night,
Capturing hearts in soft twilight.

The pages turn, and worlds collide,
Longing souls no longer hide.
In the chrysalis of the past,
Hope and pain forever last.

Glimmers of love, shadows cast,
Searching for what holds us fast.
Through the echoes, we find grace,
In the stories we embrace.

Dancing with ghosts of our desire,
Chasing dreams that lift us higher.
With each word, we build our fate,
In a tapestry we create.

Silken Threads of Connection

In the tapestry of our lives,
Silken threads of love survive.
A gentle tug, a knowing glance,
Binding hearts in a silent dance.

The fabric glows with laughter bright,
Stitched with whispers in the night.
Emotions flow like rivers wide,
Together we weave, side by side.

A single touch, the world aligns,
In the warmth, the soul defines.
Through valleys deep, we'll journey far,
Guided always by a star.

Moments cherished, softly spun,
In the tapestry, we've begun.
Each story penned, a thread so pure,
Together we'll always endure.

Through storms we face and trials we brave,
In every heart, connection a wave.
With each heartbeat, the bond grows strong,
In silken threads, we all belong.

Timeless Tangles

In shadows deep, the past entwines,
With every choice, a path defines.
Through years evolved, our spirits soar,
In timeless tangles, we explore.

Moments twist like ivy's grasp,
Holding tight, we dare to clasp.
Fates collide with gentle force,
In life's dance, we find our course.

Whispers echo through the halls,
Each decision, a silent call.
Interwoven, our hearts reside,
In tangled threads, we cannot hide.

The beauty lies in every knot,
Lessons learned, though we forgot.
In the chaos, harmony sings,
In timeless tangles, life brings.

Together woven, we explore,
The mystery of forevermore.
Each twist and turn reveals the light,
In timeless love, we find our flight.

The Bridge Between Us

In twilight's glow, we stand and share,
Two souls entwined, a love so rare.
Across the void, our laughter soars,
A bridge of dreams that ever endures.

Through storms we walk, hand in hand,
Building trust on shifting sand.
With every whisper, a promise made,
Together strong, we will not fade.

In silence deep, our hearts converse,
In every verse, we share our verse.
The paths we tread are intertwined,
A tapestry of love defined.

Through valleys low and peaks so high,
Our love shall never say goodbye.
For in your eyes, I've found my place,
A bridge that time cannot erase.

So here we stand as years unfold,
With stories new and dreams of old.
Hand in hand, we'll face the night,
Two hearts ablaze, forever bright.

Threads of Forever

In the loom of time, we weave our fate,
Two souls connected, never late.
With threads of love, we craft each day,
A tapestry that won't decay.

Through colors bold and whispers soft,
In every stitch, our dreams take off.
A fabric rich, both weak and strong,
In this embrace, we both belong.

Across the years, through joy and woe,
Threads of forever gently flow.
A guiding line through darkest nights,
Each strand a beacon, love ignites.

From the first stitch to the last seam,
We build our world, we chase the dream.
Intertwined, our spirits rise,
In this lovely weave, love never dies.

So hold me close, let's weave anew,
With every thread, I'll cherish you.
In this design, our hearts will find,
Threads of forever, so intertwined.

Mirrors of the Mind

In reflections deep, we see our truth,
Two minds entwined, recalling youth.
Through shadows cast and light that plays,
Mirrors of the mind, in endless ways.

Each thought a ripple, softly spun,
A dance of echoes, two become one.
In silent whispers, dreams align,
Revealing visions, yours and mine.

Through clarity and doubt we stride,
In tangled webs, we must confide.
A journey shared, our fears laid bare,
In the mirror's gaze, we find our care.

With every glance, we learn and grow,
In the depths of mind, our love will glow.
A spectrum wide, our hearts embrace,
Within these mirrors, we find our place.

So hold my gaze, let truth be shown,
In every thought, we are not alone.
For in this space, the heart can bind,
A love reflected, mirrors of the mind.

A Chorus of Hearts

In harmony, our hearts take flight,
A chorus sings through day and night.
With voices strong, we rise together,
Melodies weave, our hearts endeavor.

In laughter bright and tears that flow,
Each heartbeat adds to the crescendo.
The rhythm found in every glance,
A dance of love, our sweet romance.

Through every note, our story grows,
In shared embrace, our passion flows.
With every chord, our spirits soar,
A symphony that we adore.

In quiet moments, soft refrains,
Our love sings sweet through joys and pains.
Together strong, no fear or doubt,
A chorus loud, we sing it out.

So let us rise, in harmony,
With every heart, a melody.
In this great song, forever sound,
A chorus of hearts, forever bound.

Mosaic of Memories

Fragments of time, they dance and play,
Among the shadows of yesterday.
Laughter echoes in silent halls,
As the fleeting moment gently calls.

Colors blend in the mind's eye,
Cherished whispers beneath the sky.
An album filled with dreams we weave,
In the tapestry of what we believe.

Worn photographs in faded light,
Hold the stories of heart's delight.
A glance, a smile, a fleeting glance,
Forever etched in memory's dance.

Sands of time, as they flow and shift,
Hold our past, a precious gift.
Each grain a tale of love and strife,
Composing the mosaic of our life.

Heartstrings in Harmony

In the silence, hearts entwine,
Melodies sweet, like vintage wine.
Notes that linger, soft and pure,
A symphony of love, we ensure.

Fingers brush on strings of fate,
Creating rhythms that captivate.
With every beat, emotions soar,
Resonating deep at the core.

Through valleys low and mountains high,
We dance along the open sky.
With every heartbeat, every sigh,
Our loving echoes never die.

Together we write a timeless song,
Where every note feels right, never wrong.
The harmonies of our hearts will show,
In perfect sync, we ebb and flow.

Portraits of Longing

Canvas stretched with colors bright,
Yet shadows linger in the light.
Each stroke reveals a hidden sigh,
A beauty wrapped in soft goodbye.

Eyes that search for distant dreams,
In every glance, a tale redeems.
A brush of hope, a dash of fate,
Creating visions to resonate.

Among the hues of dusk and dawn,
Yearnings dance, our hearts withdrawn.
In the gallery where time stands still,
Each portrait whispers of unfulfilled.

With every gaze, a longing grows,
In silent verse, the heart just knows.
These portraits speak what words can't say,
A silent dance in shades of gray.

The Language of Caress

Soft whispers linger on the skin,
Where touch transcends, and we begin.
Fingers trace the paths of bliss,
In a world where silence is a kiss.

The gentle brush, a painter's hand,
Crafting moments, perfectly planned.
With every caress, the language flows,
In tender tones, affection grows.

Eyes entwined like branches twined,
In warmth, our spirits are aligned.
A conversation without a word,
In every heartbeat, love is stirred.

In the realm of an endless embrace,
We find our sacred, sacred space.
With each touch, we write a story,
In the language of caress, our glory.

Labyrinth of Longing

In shadows deep, we wander slow,
Through twists and turns, where heartbeats glow.
A whispered sigh, a fleeting glance,
In every corner, a hidden chance.

The walls confide, our secrets keep,
Entwined in dreams, where passions leap.
A path unknown, yet familiar too,
In this maze of hope, it's me and you.

With every step, the heart takes flight,
Through echoes soft, in the still of night.
A yearning song, the silence breaks,
In the labyrinth, our love awakes.

The walls may shift, the nooks may bend,
Yet in this journey, there's no end.
For in each turn, a truth we find,
A bond unchained, our souls defined.

So hand in hand, we'll dare to roam,
Through the labyrinth, we find our home.
With every breath, our spirits rise,
In this maze of longing, love never dies.

Cadence of Companionship

In laughter shared, our spirits play,
A melody soft, guiding our way.
With every beat, our hearts align,
In the rhythm of us, a love divine.

Through seasons change, we stand secure,
In whispers soft, our hearts endure.
A song of trust, in harmony,
The cadence of two, is meant to be.

In silence deep, our thoughts entwine,
A harmony sweet, both yours and mine.
With every glance, a story told,
In the dance of life, together bold.

With open hands, we face the night,
In shadows cast, we find the light.
Through every trial, our bond will shine,
In this cadence of love, we intertwine.

So side by side, we'll walk this road,
In every step, our hearts bestowed.
With every heartbeat, we'll rise and fall,
In the cadence of companionship, we have it all.

Whirlwind of Affection

In a dance of storms, our spirits twirl,
A tempest fierce, where feelings swirl.
With every touch, the world ignites,
In this whirlwind, our love takes flight.

Through gusts that sway, we hold on tight,
In chaos bright, our hearts take flight.
A fervent breeze that whips us near,
In the whirlwind, there's naught to fear.

With laughter high, and whispers low,
Through swirling clouds, our passions flow.
In the eye of love, where peace resides,
In this whirlwind, our joy abides.

Each moment tender, a gust, a sigh,
In the rush of love, we laugh and cry.
Through every storm, we'll find our way,
In this whirlwind of affection, come what may.

So let the winds of fate collide,
In this dance of love, we're side by side.
With hearts aflame, together we soar,
In the whirlwind of affection, forever more.

Chords of Connection

A gentle strum, the heartstrings play,
In quiet moments, come what may.
With every note, our spirits rise,
In the chords of love, the world complies.

Through melodies sweet, our laughter blends,
In the symphony, where time transcends.
A harmony forged in the fires of trust,
In the chords of connection, love is a must.

With every beat, a story flows,
In the rhythm of hearts, true essence shows.
Through highs and lows, we find our song,
In this chorus of life, we both belong.

As the music swells, we dance along,
In every embrace, we find where we belong.
With each refrain, our love ignites,
In the chords of connection, our hearts unite.

So let us play, through night and day,
In a concerto bright, come what may.
With every sound, we'll weave our tale,
In the chords of connection, love will prevail.

Luminescence of Love

In shadows' dance, we find our light,
Hand in hand, in soft twilight,
Your laughter sparkles in the air,
A glow that banishes despair.

Through silent nights, our hearts align,
Stars above, they weave and entwine,
Each tender glance, a glowing spark,
Guiding us through realms of dark.

With every heartbeat, colors blend,
A masterpiece that knows no end,
In whispered dreams, our spirits soar,
Together, forever, we explore.

In the warmth of your embrace,
I see the universe in your face,
The world ignites with every kiss,
In luminescence, we find bliss.

As twilight fades into the dawn,
Our love ignites, forever drawn,
Through time and space, we'll rise above,
In every step, the light of love.

Infinite Intersections

Paths converge in endless grace,
With each turn, a new embrace,
In every glance, a story told,
Of hearts entwined, brave and bold.

A dance of souls, a fateful chance,
Caught in the rhythm of a trance,
With every step, the world unfolds,
In sacred truths, our journey molds.

Where laughter meets the quiet night,
The stars ignite, a guiding light,
In the chaos, we find our way,
Through infinite crossroads, come what may.

In every whisper, a promise lies,
To seek the truth beneath the skies,
Together we'll forge what time will not end,
In endless circles, hand in hand we blend.

Through fleeting moments, we collide,
In every heartbeat, love's our guide,
With every intersection, we see,
Life's beautiful web holds you and me.

Whispers of Affection

In evening's hush, soft words arise,
A melody beneath the skies,
Gentle breezes carry our song,
In every note, where we belong.

With tender glances, secrets shared,
In silent moments, love declared,
Caressing dreams, like petals fall,
In whispers sweet, we have it all.

Through tangled thoughts, our hearts will weave,
A tapestry of love, believe,
In fleeting moments, time stands still,
In every breath, a deeper thrill.

As starlit night enfolds the day,
Our souls shall dance, come what may,
In quiet corners of the night,
We find the peace, our purest light.

In every whisper, love's caress,
A gentle touch, eternal bliss,
With every sigh, our world expands,
In each embrace, fate's gentle hands.

Canvas of Hearts

In colors bright, our passions bloom,
A canvas filled with sweet perfume,
Each stroke a tale of love confessed,
In vibrant hues, our hearts find rest.

With brush in hand, we shade and blend,
In perfect harmony, we mend,
Your laughter paints the skies above,
In every line, the art of love.

On this canvas, dreams take flight,
In soft pastels, we find our light,
With every hue, the world we share,
A masterpiece beyond compare.

From silver moons to golden rays,
Each moment captured, love portrays,
A landscape rich with memories dear,
In every color, we hold you near.

In our gallery, time stands still,
A painted promise, love will thrill,
Through every season, hearts will gleam,
In the canvas of love, we dream.

Crystalized Gleams

In twilight's soft embrace we stand,
Wonders of light within our hand.
Shimmers dance on edges bright,
A world transformed by fading light.

Each drop a tale, a break in time,
Sparkling stories in perfect rhyme.
Whispers echo, secrets shared,
In crystalized gleams, we're unprepared.

Nature's gems in varied hues,
A fleeting glimpse of morning views.
As colors blend, they come alive,
A radiant pulse where dreams contrive.

Hold them close, these moments rare,
A treasure found in fragile air.
Drifting softly, they slip away,
Yet in our hearts, they choose to stay.

With every glint a spark ignites,
Illuminating darkest nights.
In crystalized gleams, we'll find our way,
Guided by light, come what may.

Reflections of Reverie

A mirror pools of tranquil dreams,
Where thoughts float softly like moonbeams.
In gentle waves, our wishes glide,
We dance with shadows side by side.

Each image tells a story bold,
In gilded frames, our lives unfold.
The past whispers in silken tones,
In this reverie, we find our bones.

A canvas painted with desire,
The colors spark a timeless fire.
Through fleeting moments, we escape,
In mirrored worlds, we reshape our fate.

Thoughts drift like feathered sighs,
Beneath the starlit, vastened skies.
In echoes of what might have been,
Reflections glisten with a sheen.

We gather dreams with tender care,
In the solace of the dreamer's air.
Reflections fade, yet still inspire,
A loving heart a pure desire.

Trails of Trust

In forest deep, where shadows creep,
We weave a path, our secrets keep.
With every step, we pave the way,
In trails of trust, our hearts convey.

The leaves whisper stories shared,
In gentle breezes, we are bared.
Each moment holds a strength anew,
In trails of trust, we will pursue.

Through winding paths, we walk as one,
Underneath the warming sun.
Hand in hand, we brave the night,
In trails of trust, we find our light.

In laughter's echo, in silent tears,
We conquer doubts, dissolve our fears.
Each twist and turn, a lesson learned,
In trails of trust, our spirits burned.

No mountain high, no river wide,
Can break the bond we choose to bide.
With every heartbeat, stronger we grow,
In trails of trust, our love will flow.

The Colors We Create

In palette bright, we splash and play,
Crafting hues that dance and sway.
Each stroke a tale, a bold embrace,
In the colors we create, we trace.

Through vibrant reds and azure skies,
Imagination's art never dies.
With laughter's tint, we paint the days,
In the colors we create, our hearts blaze.

Every shade tells stories true,
Of dreams fulfilled and skies of blue.
Blending moments, both dark and light,
In the colors we create, pure delight.

As sun dips low, the canvas glows,
Rendering beauty through highs and lows.
In every hue, our voices sing,
In the colors we create, we spring.

Together we weave our visions free,
A masterpiece of you and me.
Brightening shadows with our fate,
In the colors we create, we celebrate.

Serenade of Souls

In the twilight's soft glow, we dance,
Whispers of dreams in a fleeting trance.
Hearts beat as one, in a timeless flow,
Love's tender song, a beautiful show.

Stars watch from above, a celestial gaze,
Guiding our steps through the night's maze.
Each note we play, so sweet and bright,
A serenade soft, to warm the night.

Mosaic of Emotions

Fragments of laughter, pieces of pain,
Colors collide in a vivid rain.
Joy interlaces with sorrow's thread,
A canvas alive with all that we've said.

Each hue a memory, each shade a sigh,
Crafting a story as seasons fly by.
In this tapestry, we softly weave,
An intricate pattern, one heart to believe.

Echoes of a Gentle Embrace

In the hush of the night, your touch lingers,
Warming my soul with your tender fingers.
Every heartbeat a whisper, soft and clear,
In your gentle embrace, I find no fear.

Moments suspended, in time they thrall,
Wrapped in this love, I am given my all.
Like waves on the shore, our spirits entwined,
In the echo of silence, our souls aligned.

Threads of Intimacy

Woven together, our lives intertwine,
In whispers and glances, a love so divine.
Each secret shared, a thread so fine,
Binding our hearts in the softest design.

Through laughter and tears, we craft and we sew,
An intricate quilt, where tenderness grows.
In the fabric of moments, both fragile and bold,
Our story unfolds, in colors untold.

Notes from the Heartstrings

In the quiet night, whispers dwell,
Echoes of dreams, a silken spell.
Threads of emotion weave through the air,
Softly they linger, without a care.

Promises made, in laughter and tears,
Carved in the silence, confirmed through fears.
Each note a heartbeat, pulsing with grace,
Binding our souls in a warm embrace.

Moments like music, dancing in light,
Filling the shadows, igniting the night.
Harmony whispers in every sigh,
A symphony played, just you and I.

Chords of affection play loud and soft,
Lifting us up, like a gentle loft.
Together we strum, on life's fragile stage,
Crafting our story, page by page.

Love is a melody, timeless and true,
A song of together, always anew.
With each note, we find where we belong,
Notes from the heartstrings, our endless song.

Enigma of Us

In the dance of shadows, we find our way,
Two wandering souls, both lost and yet brave.
Mysteries hide in the lines of our past,
Fleeting moments, too fragile to last.

Every glance shared, a puzzle unclear,
Fragments of laughter, tinged with the fear.
What do you hold in the depths of your gaze?
A labyrinth woven, in fog and in haze?

Words left unspoken, linger in air,
Connecting our hearts in a tender despair.
The enigma deepens with each fleeting thought,
A maze of emotions, so easily caught.

Hands that entwine, yet tremble apart,
Searching for answers that tease at the heart.
What is the truth in this game that we play?
An enigma of us, in shades of gray.

Through the confusion, a warmth still ignites,
In the silence, we find what feels right.
Together we wander this path made for two,
In the enigma of us, I discover you.

Songs of Serendipity

Under starlit skies, fate softly sings,
Whispers of joy, the warmth that it brings.
Paths intertwined, as if drawn by fate,
Moments collide, it's never too late.

Every turn taken, a melody sweet,
Life's little surprises, no map can compete.
In the unexpected, happiness flows,
Gifts of the heart, only serendipity knows.

Laughter erupts from the mundane grind,
A spark in the silence, awakening mind.
Songs that we hum on a road rarely planned,
An echo of chance, life's gracious hand.

Smiles shared with strangers, warmth in the air,
Connections unwritten, tender and rare.
Each note a reminder, joy's fleeting bliss,
Caught in the warmth of a serendipitous kiss.

So we'll dance through the days, hearts open wide,
Searching for magic, with love as our guide.
With every sweet song, a story we weave,
In the arms of fate, we learn to believe.

Raindrops of Reverence

Softly they fall, whispers from high,
Raindrops of reverence, kissing the sky.
Nature's sweet hymn in a gentle refrain,
Washing away all of yesterday's pain.

Each droplet a prayer, pure and divine,
Cleansing the world with a rhythm so fine.
A dance on the leaves, a song on the ground,
Life's tender heartbeat, in silence profound.

They gather and pool, like thoughts in our heads,
Reflecting our dreams and the paths that we've tread.
In puddles of solace, we find who we are,
Beneath the soft rhythm, we reach for the stars.

In the embrace of the storm, we find our strength,
Resilience blooms, as we go to great lengths.
With every drop falling, a promise we make,
To honor the moment, let our hearts wake.

So let's dance in the rain, as the world comes alive,
In raindrops of reverence, together we thrive.
Each splash tells a story of love and of grace,
In nature's sweet symphony, we find our place.

Lullabies of Luxurious Affection

In whispers of silk, soft dreams arise,
Lavished in gold, beneath starlit skies.
Crimson petals dance in gentle embrace,
Love's tender echo, time cannot erase.

As moonlight kisses, the night blooms bright,
Warmth of your presence ignites pure light.
Fingers entwined, a promise we weave,
In lullabies sweet, we dare to believe.

A tapestry woven with threads of delight,
Moments like gems, in the heart take flight.
Soft lullabies hum, a love song so deep,
In the cradle of passion, together we sleep.

The night sky whispers secrets untold,
In the arms of affection, we cherish our gold.
Beneath every star, our love softly glows,
In the lull of the night, true devotion flows.

Wrapped in the warmth of a silken cocoon,
Our laughter rises like the sun at noon.
In luxurious depths, our hearts intertwine,
In the lullabies sung, forever you're mine.

Sighs in Shadows

Beneath the veil of twilight's embrace,
Sorrowful whispers fade without trace.
In the depths of darkness, memories creep,
Sighs in the shadows, secrets we keep.

Moonlight flickers on a heart grown cold,
Echoes of laughter, a story retold.
Time lingers softly, a haunting refrain,
In sighs of the shadows, we feel the pain.

The night wraps around like a shroud of mist,
Dreams intertwined, too precious to risk.
Wandering thoughts in the quietest hour,
Sighs in the shadows, a lingering power.

Years slip away in the hush of the night,
The weight of lost love, a painful delight.
In the corners of dusk, where memories flow,
Sighs in the shadows, forever we know.

Every heartbeat echoes, a tale still alive,
In the silence of dark, our spirits revive.
As dawn breaks the spell, the shadows will fade,
But the sighs in the night, forever will stay.

Sails of Sentiment

On gentle waves, our hearts set the sail,
Through tempest and calm, we will prevail.
Carried by winds of hope and of dreams,
In the sea of emotion, our love brightly beams.

Stars guide our journey on waters unknown,
In the depths of longing, our spirits have grown.
With every rippling wave, we find our way,
Sails of sentiment, here we shall stay.

Beneath the vast sky, we gather the light,
With whispers of love that dance in the night.
In the arms of the ocean, we learn to be free,
Sails of sentiment, you and me, we.

With horizons ahead, our compass aligned,
Together we sail, our hearts intertwined.
Through storms and through calm, our hearts do prevail,
On this vast journey, with sails we set sail.

No treasure is greater than love's endless tides,
Through the waves of our journey, our passion abides.
As we chart our course on this beautiful sea,
Sails of sentiment, forever we'll be.

Awakening the Heart

In the hush of dawn, new light gently breaks,
Awakening whispers, the spirit awakes.
With each tender moment, the heart learns to soar,
Through the veil of dreams, we discover much more.

The petals of morning, in sunlight they bloom,
Chasing away shadows, dispelling the gloom.
With every heartbeat, the world comes alive,
Awakening the heart, our souls start to thrive.

In the dance of the day, we find our own tune,
As the sun paints the sky with the colors of June.
Hand in hand, together, we'll journey so far,
Awakening the heart, like a bright guiding star.

Each memory cherished, each laugh a sweet song,
Love's tender embrace helps us all to belong.
Through moments of joy, as the day stretches wide,
Awakening the heart, with you by my side.

With gratitude filling these beautiful hours,
We bloom like the flowers, in love's gentle showers.
In the stillness of life, your light is my chart,
Fostering dreams that awaken the heart.

Milton Keynes UK
Ingram Content Group UK Ltd.
UKHW021001241024
450188UK00012B/515